THE MEANING OF
SUFFERING

KÜBLER-ROSS IN PERSON

THE MEANING OF SUFFERING

ELISABETH KÜBLER-ROSS, M.D.

EDITED BY GÖRAN GRIP, M.D.

STATION HILL OPENINGS

BARRYTOWN, LTD.

Copyright © 1997 by Elisabeth Kübler-Ross.

All rights reserved. No part of this book may be reproduced or utilized in any form or by any means, electronic or mechanical, including photocopying, recording, or by any information storage and retrieval system, without permission in writing from the publisher.

Published under the Station Hill Openings imprint by Barrytown, Ltd., Barrytown, N.Y. 12507.

Distributed by Consortium Book Sales & Distribution, Inc. 1045 Westgate Drive, Saint Paul, MN 55114-1065.

Text and cover design by Susan Quasha.

The talk in this book has been excerpted from *Death is Of Vital Importance*, Copyright by Elisabeth Kübler-Ross, Station Hill Press, 1995.

A Swedish version of *Death is Of Vital Importance* has been published by Bokförlaget Natur och Kultur under the title *Döden är livsviktig: Om livet, döden och livet efter döden*, Copyright 1991 by Elisabeth Kübler-Ross.

Library of Congress Cataloging-in-Publication Data

Kübler-Ross, Elisabeth.
    The meaning of suffering / Elisabeth Kübler-Ross ; edited by Göran Grip.
        p. cm. – (Kübler-Ross in person)
    Excerpted from: Death is of vital importance, 1995.
    ISBN 1-886449-24-4 (lg. Print)
    1. Death. 2. Life. 3. Future life. 4. Spiritual life.
    I. Grip, Göran. II. Title. III. Series: Kübler-Ross, Elisabeth.
    Kübler-Ross in person.
    [BD444.K795 1997]
    155.9'37—dc21   96-48975
                                                     CIP

Printed in the United States of America

Contents

Maidanek 5

The Symbolic Language 14

Children Losing a Relative 23

Jaimie's Brother 25

Lorrie 27

The Boy in San Diego 42

Interpretation of Children's Drawings 44

Liz 51

Dougy 63

The Meaning of Suffering 74

About This Book

Elisabeth Kübler-Ross' words, spoken at the spur of the moment, have been edited here with the aim of creating a readable text. We have taken pains, however, to preserve the quality of immediate presence that is characterized by the author's special magnetism, the power of direct address to a live audience for which she is renowned. We think there is a special meaning in presenting Elisabeth Kübler-Ross "live" on the subject of death and dying — and that this is a key to her message.

This book has been adapted from Elisabeth Kübler-Ross' tape-recorded lecture, *Death is of Vital Importance*, delivered in Stockholm, Sweden, in 1980.

The Meaning of Suffering

I was born in Switzerland in a typically Swiss family, very thrifty like most Swiss, very authoritarian like most Swiss, very... unliberal, if you can say that. We had all the material things in the world and we had loving parents.

But I was born an "unwanted" child. Not that my parents didn't want a child. They wanted a girl very badly, but a pretty, beautiful, ten-pound girl. They did not expect triplets and when I came, I was only two pounds. I was very ugly and had no hair, and I was a terribly, terribly big disappointment to my parents.

Fifteen minutes later the second one came, and after another twenty minutes a six and a half pound baby came, and *then* they were very happy. But they would have liked to give two of us back.

So I had the tragedy of being born a triplet. That is the biggest tragedy, that I don't wish my worst enemy. If you are raised an identical triplet, it is very peculiar because you can literally drop dead and nobody would know the difference. I had the feeling that I had to prove all my life that even I, a two-pound nothing, was worth something. I had to work really hard for that, in the same way that some blind people think that they have to work ten times as hard as everybody else in order to keep their job. I had to prove very hard that I was worth living.

I had to be born and raised in this way in order to do this work. It took me fifty years to understand that. It took me fifty years to realize that there are no coincidences in life, not even the circumstances of our birth, and that the things we regard as tragedies are not really tragedies unless we choose to make tragedies out of them. Because we can also choose to regard them as chances for us, opportunities to grow, and then we see that they are challenges and hints that we may need to change our lives.

When you are at the end of your life and look back, not at the easy days but at the tough days, at the windstorms of life, you see that the tough days are the ones that really made you what you are today. It is like... somebody said once, "It's like putting a rock in a tumbler. You have the choice to come out crashed or polished."

And to be raised as a triplet is such a challenge: for years and years and years knowing, being totally aware of the fact that my own mother and father didn't know whether they talked to me or to my sister, being aware that my teachers didn't know whether I deserved an A or an F, and therefore always gave us C's.

One day my sister went on her first date. She was in love like a typical teenager who is in love for the first time. The second time the boy invited her she became very sick and just couldn't go and was heartbroken. Then I said to her, "Don't worry. If you really can't go and you are heartbroken and afraid that you are going to lose him, I will go for you *(amusement from audience)*. And he will never know the difference."

I asked her how far she went. And I went on the date for her, and her boyfriend never noticed the difference *(amusement from audience)*.

You may think now, looking back, that it's a funny story, but for a teenager like me it was very tragic to think that you could be in love with somebody, that you could go out with him, and that you were *totally* and completely and absolutely replaceable. Sometimes I even wonder if I am not my sister.

I needed to learn this lesson early in life, because after this incident, when I realized that my sister's boyfriend didn't know the difference between her and me, I probably made the most difficult choice in my whole life and that was to leave Switzerland, to leave my family, to leave the security of my home. I went on a trip through post war Europe. I also came to Sweden where I gave a workshop for workshop leaders.

Maidanek

I ended up in Maidanek in Poland, in a concentration camp where I saw train loads of baby shoes of murdered children, train loads of human hair. To read about this in books is one thing, but to stand there and see the crematories and smell it with your own nose is something quite different.

I was nineteen and I came from a country where there are no windstorms. We have no race problem, no poverty, and we have had no war for 760 years. I didn't know what life was. In this place, suddenly all the windstorms of life came flooding down on me. After an experience like that, one will never ever be the same person again. And I bless this day. Without that windstorm I would not be in this work today.

I asked myself: how can grownups, men and women like you and me, kill 960,000 innocent children and at the same time worry about their own children at home having chicken-pox?

And then I went to the barracks where the children had spent the last night of their life, not knowing why but, I guess, in search of messages or cues how these children had faced death. The children had scratched symbols into the barrack walls with their finger nails or a piece of rock or chalk, and the most frequent one of them were butterflies.

I saw those butterflies. I was very young. I was very ignorant. I had no idea why five, six, seven, eight, nine-year-old children who were taken away from home, from their parents, from the security of their homes and schools into cattle cars, and shipped to Auschwitz and Buchenwald and Maidanek, why these children should see butterflies. It took me a quarter of a century to find the answer.

Maidanek was the beginning of my work.

In Maidanek I found a young Jewish girl who stayed there instead of leaving. I couldn't understand why. She had lost her grandparents, her parents and all her brothers and sisters in the gas chamber in the concentration camp. The gas chamber had been filled and then they couldn't squeeze another person into it, and so she was spared.

In my horror I asked her, "What in the world are you doing here? Why do you stay here in this place of inhumanity?" She said, "During the last few weeks of the concentration camp I swore to myself that I was going to survive to do nothing but tell the world of all the horrors of the Nazis and the concentration camps. Then the liberation army came. I looked at those people and I said to myself: 'No. If I would do that, I would be no better than Hitler himself.' Because what else would I then do but to plant even more seeds of hate and negativity in the world? But if I can truly believe that nobody gets more than they can take, that we are never alone, that I can acknowledge the tragedy and the nightmare of Maidanek and leave it behind, if I can touch one single human life and turn it away from negativity, from hate, from revenge, from bitterness into one that can serve and love and care, then it may be worthwhile and I deserved to survive."

Negativity can only feed on negativity and will then continue to grow like a cancer grows. But we also have the choice to accept what happened as a sad and horrible reality, which is gone, which has passed, and which cannot be changed. And she made that choice.

What she *could* change, however, was what she was going to do, what she was going to make out of all that had happened. And so she decided to stay in this horrible place of horrible sights and smells.

She and I went to the barracks. She and I discovered the butterflies. She and I began to talk like two young people. She and I began to philosophize together about life and death. And she was the one who said to me, "Don't you believe, Elisabeth, that in all of us there is a Hitler?" She and I realized at a very young age that it *really* depends only on our own courage to look at our own negativity and our own negative potential, if we are to become serving, loving human beings. Because in all of us there is *also* the potential of becoming a Mother Theresa.

⚬⚬⚬

We parted ways. I went back to Switzerland. I studied medicine. My dream was to go somewhere in Africa or India and become a doctor like Albert Schweitzer. But two weeks before I was supposed to leave for India, I was notified that the whole project there had fallen through. And instead of the jungles of India I ended up in the jungles of Brooklyn, New York. I married an American, who took me to the one place in the world that was at the bottom of my list of places where I ever wanted to live: New York City, the biggest jungle in the world. I was *very* unhappy.

As a foreign doctor in New York it is impossible to find a good residency in June, and so I ended up in a Manhattan State Hospital with chronic, hopeless, schizophrenic patients. I had trouble understanding their English. When they talked Schizophrenese to me they could as well have been talking Chinese. I didn't know any psychiatry. I was a good country doctor but I was not a psychiatrist.

Not really knowing any psychiatry, and being very lonely and miserable and unhappy, and not wanting to make my new husband unhappy, I opened up to the patients. I identified with their misery and their loneliness and their desperation.

And suddenly my patients started to talk. People who hadn't talked for twenty years started to verbalize and share their feelings. Suddenly I knew that I was not alone in my misery, though *my* misery wasn't half as bad as living in a state hospital. For two years I did nothing but live and work with these patients, sharing every Hanukkah, Christmas, Passover and Easter with them, just to share their loneliness, not knowing much psychiatry, the theoretical psychiatry that one ought to know. I barely understood their

English, but we loved each other. We really cared.

I began to listen to them. Not to their language but to their nonverbal, symbolic communications. Then I realized that the only thing that turned those people on, that made them behave and react like human beings, were two things, both of them very unhealthy but all the same very human. It was cigarettes and Coca Cola.

Only when they received cigarettes and Coke did they show any human reactions and responses. Many of them had been in the state hospital locked up worse than animals for up to twenty years.

And so again, I had to make a choice. I took the cigarettes and the Coke away from them. That was very hard for me, because I am a softy. I told them that if they wanted to learn self-respect and regain some degree of dignity and self-worth and become human again, they had to *earn* their benefits.

And in one week those people, who really didn't respond to anything, were all dressed up. They had combed their hair, were wearing shoes and stood in line to go to workshop to do piece work in order to earn their own benefits, their cigarettes and Coca Cola.

We did very simple things like that. I really loved those people, because when I grew up I knew what it was like to have everything and still to have nothing. Being raised as a triplet in a well-to-do household where I was loved, where I had all the material things, I still had absolutely nothing because nobody knew that I existed as an individual human being.

So instead of talking about the schizophrenic in room seventeen and the manic depressive in room fifty-three, I knew those people by name, I knew their idiosyncrasies, I knew their likes and dislikes. And they began to respond to me.

Two years later we were able to discharge ninety-four percent of these so-called hopeless, chronic schizophrenics, not on welfare but self-supporting in New York City. I was very proud of it.

I think that the greatest gift that those patients gave me was to teach me that there is something beyond drugs, beyond electroshock treatment, and beyond the science of medicine; that it is with real love and care that you can truly help people and make many, many people well.

What I'm trying to say to you is that knowledge helps, but knowledge *alone* is not going to help anybody. If you do not use your head and your heart and your soul, you are not going to help a single human being. In all my work with patients, I learned that whether they are chronic schizophrenics, severely retarded children, or dying patients, each one has a purpose. Each one cannot only learn and be helped by you, but can actually become your teacher. That is true of six-month old retarded babies who can't speak. That is also true of hopeless schizophrenic patients who behave like animals when you see them for the first time.

The Symbolic Language

The second gift my schizophrenic patients gave me was that I learned a language without which I would not have been able to work with dying children. That language is the symbolic, universal language that people all over the world use when they are in a crisis. If you are raised naturally — not normally because normally means terribly unnaturally — you would never have to read books on death and dying in order to work with dying patients, because you would be able to learn what needs to be done the way I learned it in Manhattan State Hospital. I always say — half joking, because I am serious about it — that the only honest people left on this earth are psychotics, young children and dying patients. And if you use these three kinds of people — and I mean "use" in a positive sense — if you can learn to hear, really hear them, they will teach you what we call the symbolic language.

People in pain, people in shock, people in numbness, people who are overwhelmed with a tragedy that they believe is beyond their comprehension, beyond their ability to cope with, use this language. Dying children, who are faced with their imminent death know it even if they have never been taught it. The symbolic language is a universal language, and it is used by all people all over the world.

There is no one dying, whether he is five or ninety-five, who does not know that he is dying. And the question is not: do I tell him that he is dying? The question is: can I hear him?

The patient may tell you for example, "I'll not be around for your birthday in July." It is good if you can hear that without your own need making you say, "Oh, don't talk like that. You are going to get well," because that would interrupt the communication between the patient and you, because the patient would understand that you are not ready to hear, and so you literally shut her up and she will feel very lonely.

But if you have no issues about death and dying, if you can acknowledge that this woman knows internally that she is close to death, then you sit with her and touch her, and you say, "Is there anything I can do for you, Grandma?" or whatever.

I was told of a young woman who was visiting her old grandmother. The old woman took the ring off her finger and gave it to her young granddaughter without saying a word. That is nonverbal, symbolic language. She simply put it on her granddaughter's finger. And this granddaughter didn't say, "Oh, Grandma, don't do that. You love this ring. I want you to keep it." Instead she said, "You really want *me* to have it?" And Grandma made like this: *(Elisabeth demonstrates how Grandma is nodding).* And then the granddaughter said, "Why don't you..." and then she stopped what she intended to say which was, "Why don't you wait and give it to me for Christmas," because she immediately knew that Grandma must know that she would not be here at Christmas any more. And

Grandma was very, very happy that she had the privilege to give the ring to her. She died two days before Christmas. That is symbolic, nonverbal language.

⚬━━━⚬

But very often the patients do *not* talk to you in plain English or plain Swedish. Many people feel your anxiety when you visit them. That makes them start talking about the weather. Not because they are interested in the weather, of course, but because they sense your anxiety and therefore keep their problems to themselves. The reason for this is that they don't want to add to *your* anxiety, because they are afraid that if they do, then maybe you will walk out on them and won't visit them any more.

When people try to convey to you their own awareness of a terminal illness, or any other tragedy for that matter, they will basically use three languages: one of them in Sweden would be plain Swedish. If the patients tell you when you are visiting them, "I know I have cancer. I am not getting out of this hospital any more," those are the people that you hear, those are the people that you help, those are the people that you respond to because they make it easy for you. They initiate your communication, they call a baby by its name. Those are the people that do *not* need your help. Because those terminally ill patients who can talk in plain Swedish or English about their own cancer and their own dying are the people who have already transcended their biggest fear, the fear of death. Actually they end up helping *you* and not the other way around. You may never admit it, but they are really *your* therapists, they are a gift to *you*. Those are not the people I am talking about tonight.

The people who need your help, who need it desperately, are the ones who are in a state of shock and numbness, people who are not prepared for the windstorms of life, people who have been pampered in life and for whom everything has been easy and smooth, people who come from families where they were protected from all hardships. Those people have been raised in a greenhouse. Sooner or later the windstorms hit them, and they are not prepared for them, like the parents who lost all their children to different forms of cancer within six months and were left childless. They were in such pain, such disbelief that this could happen to them, that they could not talk about it in plain English. And so they turned to the symbolic language instead. I beg you to learn this language so that you will be able to hear them.

There are two kinds of symbolic language: the symbolic nonverbal and the symbolic verbal language. Both are universal languages that you can use all over the world. And once you understand this language, which is the language that children use almost exclusively, then you will never have to guess, you will never have to gamble, and you will begin to understand that every single dying child, every single dying adult knows — not always consciously but subconsciously — that they are dying. They will share with you the one thing they need to share, and that is their unfinished business.

Some of you may know what a "parable" is. Jesus was very smart. He knew that He wanted to teach a lot of people what He came to teach. But the population wasn't ready; at least lots of them were not ready. And so He used parables, knowing that those who were ready to hear would hear. And the others are still scratching their heads two thousand years later *(amusement from audience)*. That is exactly the language that my dying children use when they pick *you* — and they do pick with whom they try that language. It may be a nurse's aide or somebody whom they think will be able to understand. Three-, four-year-old children look at you and they look through you and they know whether you can take it or whether you immediately will say, "Oh, children don't know about such things. He is just talking."

They use a language very similar to parables, a symbolic language, and if you nod when you don't know what they are talking about, you are very quickly written off as a phony-baloney. If you on the other hand understand that they are trying to tell you something but you have limited experience, then you might say, "You are trying to tell me something, but I'm not sure what it is. Say it again!" Then they will rephrase it in two, three, four or ten different variations until you do understand.

Most of the time it takes no more than one house call to help families and patients to evaluate — in a way to diagnose — their unfinished business and to help them get rid of it so they can move on and face their imminent death with peace and serenity and absence of fear and pain.

When a patient uses the symbolic language, it means that he is testing you out to see if you are ready for whatever he needs you for. Young children use almost exclusively the symbolic, nonverbal language. And the simplest, most beautiful, most helpful language that children use are drawings.

Susan Bach, a Jungian analyst from London, developed a method of looking at children's spontaneous drawings, children in Zurich at the hospital where I worked for fifteen years. She asked the children, who all had brain tumors, to draw a spontaneous picture, and then she discovered that they all revealed in their drawings their awareness of their pathology and even the location of the brain tumor.

And when she learned to analyze the drawings, she began to realize that the children not only were aware of what was happening inside their bodies but they also very often revealed how and when they were going to die.

When we have children who have leukemia, cancer or other illnesses, we ask them to draw a picture, and so they reveal their own inner sub-conscious awareness of their illness. Using the symbolic nonverbal language, we help them to finish their unfinished business and then they can help their own Mommies and Daddies to come to grips with their impending death.

Some of you have seen my book *To Live Until We Say Good Bye* and have seen the picture that five-year-old Jamie drew of a purple balloon floating up into the sky. Purple is the color of spirituality. Her concept of death was that in the very immediate future she would be a spirit floating up into the sky.

Children Losing a Relative

(Question from audience, "I would like to hear about children and their reactions after having lost a parent.") Children will react to the death of a parent depending on how they were raised before the death occurred. If parents have no fear of death, if they have not protected their children but shared with them, for example, the death of a pet or the death of a Grandma, and if they have been allowed to participate in the care of their dying parent at home and also to go to the funeral, then you will have no problems with children.

This is one of the main reasons why we take young mothers and fathers home to die. The youngest child may be responsible for picking the favorite music of Mommy. Another child may be responsible for bringing tea. A third one may be responsible for something else. In this way the children *participate* in the care of the dying mother or father. When the time comes when the mother can no longer speak and when she goes into a coma during the last few days of her life, the children can still touch her, love her and hold her.

Then the children can be told that Mommy is in a coma like in a cocoon, that she is still very much alive and that she can hear everything they say. She can even listen to music. But she can no longer talk or respond. If the children are allowed to participate in this process, they will have an incredibly beautiful learning experience.

But if the mother is in a hospital or in an intensive care unit, especially in the United States where children are not allowed to come into the hospital, the children will have terrible nightmares about what they think that we are doing to their

Mommy. And if on top of this they are not allowed to come to the funeral, then they will have a lot of fears and a lot of unfinished business, maybe for many years to come.

Our favorite motto is: *Should you shield the canyons from the windstorms, you would never see the beauty of their carvings.* That means that you should not shield your children, that you should not "protect" them, because you cannot protect them anyway. The only thing you will achieve is to protect yourself, while you prevent your children from getting an opportunity to grow and to prepare themselves for life.

Jamie's brother

Siblings have the biggest problem when you work with dying children, and the beautiful example that you can look at is in *To Live Until We Say Good-bye* where five-year-old Jamie, whom I mentioned before, died of a brain stem tumor. We were able to take her home. Her eight-year-old brother was allowed to participate in the care of his sister. He would come home from school, would very matter of factly say to his classmates that he had to go to work now, he would switch the oxygen on and very gently give her some oxygen. Then he would hop off the bed and when he would see that she needed some suctioning, with incredible love and tenderness, he suctioned her.

When she died he had no grief work whatsoever but only grief.

When the book came out with the photographs of him and his dying sister in it, I naturally went to show it to him, wondering how he would react to it. First he only looked at his own photographs, which is what all of us do, although we pretend that we look at the other pictures too *(laughter)*. When he had approved of his own photographs, he then looked at the whole chapter about his sister. His very beautiful response to it was, "I'm very glad that this came out in the form of a book. Because if my classmates lose a brother or a sister they can look at *my* book and know what they will have to do." He had a tremendous sense of pride and achievement and did not feel neglected and rejected like a great, great percentage of brothers and sister of dying children do.

When we have children whose mommy or daddy is dying, and the family asks "How in the world do we prepare the children?" you simply ask the children to draw a picture for you and then they go on to tell you how much they know about mommy's or daddy's immediate or imminent death. I will give you a practical example of this:

Lorrie

We had a school teacher who called us one day and described a first grader who had been doing wonderfully when school started, but started deteriorating rapidly a few months later. She couldn't understand why. She then called the child's home and was told by a very angry aunt that the child's mother was dying of cancer, had been in a hospital in a coma for two weeks, and was expected to die any day.

The teacher naturally asked the aunt if the children — the girl had a sister who was one year younger than her — were prepared for their mother's death. She said no. Not only had nobody told the children, but they had not seen their father for the last two weeks because, since the mother had gone into a coma, the young husband had been going to work earlier and earlier every morning to go straight to the hospital from work to be with his dying wife. By the time he came home, his two children were always asleep.

The teacher then very correctly said: "Somebody needs to talk to those children before it happens," and the aunt very angrily said, "Then *you* talk to them! But if you do it, do it now, because tomorrow it may be too late." Then she hung up on that poor teacher. Teachers have no preparation for this kind of work either.

The teacher phoned me and asked if I could help her. I told her that she could bring the children to my house after school under one condition, and that was that she stay with us in order to see what I was going to do with the children so the next time she would be able to do it herself. And she came.

I see all my dying patients in house calls, and any relatives have to come to my home for purely economical reasons. All the children who can walk, I see in my kitchen. I don't have a doctor's office because it is so scary for the children. I do not see them in the living room either. I see them in the kitchen because my kitchen has a fireplace and in Chicago, where it is sometimes 40 below zero, it is very nice to sit next to a fireplace.

I do something very 'horrible' and anti-holistic. I always serve Coca Cola and doughnuts *(laughter from audience)*. This is the unhealthiest food you can serve a child and I am aware of that as a physician. And I will tell you why I do that.

These are children who already have not been told the truth about their mother's condition. They already do not trust grown ups. They already are deteriorating in school. This means that they are very troubled and that they have no one to honestly communicate with. You can easily understand what would happen to such a distrustful kindergarten child or first grader if the teacher after school took them to a psychiatrist's private home and fed them with strange wheat germs or bean sprouts (*amusement in audience*).

Instead we give them what they are most comfortable with. Whether this is healthy or not healthy is totally and completely and absolutely irrelevant at *this* time. It is very important that you hear that. Because we would be misusing our authority and our position if we tried to convert them at this time to healthier food habits. We grownups have a tendency to do that and the children turn us off, correctly so.

A year later maybe, when these children are my friends because we have helped each other through a very difficult time, they might be willing to hear me. Then I will invite them again to my kitchen and we can cook or bake some health foods together.

I have to say that because in the past when I didn't explain why I gave them Coke and doughnuts, I got incredibly hostile letters from people, and I don't need any more of those (laughter from audience).

We usually sit down at the kitchen table with the children, and while they nibble on their doughnuts and drink their Coca Cola, I ask them to draw a picture. I give them a box of Crayola, and in two minutes I know that these children know. Then we can talk openly about it, and half an hour later they leave my house and they are OK, and it is *that* simple.

What this first grader drew was very beautiful. She drew a stick figure with enormous legs — bright red is always a color of danger — and next to it a kind of

Indian design. Before finishing it, she crossed it out very angrily, again with red which is anger and pain.

I looked at the stick figure who had totally distorted legs and said, "I wonder if that is your mommy." She curtly said, "Yes."

I said, "My God, a mommy with legs like this must have trouble walking." She looked at me like she was testing me out, and she said, "My mommy's legs are so bad that she will never again walk with us in the park."

Then the teacher interfered — they always interfere *(amusement in audience)* — and said, "No, Dr. Ross, that is not true. Her mother is full of cancer. The only part of her body that is not affected by the cancer are her legs." And I said, "Thank you. But I don't want *your* reality. I need the child's reality." She understood what I meant.

Then I made a mistake. I went back to the child and said, "Lorrie, your mommy's legs must be horrible." And *very* annoyed she said, "I *told* you that my mommy's legs are so bad that she will never again walk with us in the park." Like, "Don't you hear?" *Then* I heard her.

Then I asked her about this funny Indian figure. She wouldn't tell me.

There are some tricks in this work that you will learn by trial and error. If you want a child to tell you the truth all you need to do is to guess wrong. Sooner or later they get tired of your stupid questions and tell you the truth *(laughter from audience).*

But you cannot fake it. If I had known what this was and if I would have faked ignorance, the child would have looked through me instantly. But I really didn't know what that figure symbolized, so I guessed all sorts of things that were all wrong. And then, very annoyed, she said, "No, that's a tipped over table." I said, "A tipped over table?" And she said, "Yes, my mommy will never again have dinner with us at the kitchen table."

If a child tells you "never again" three times in three minutes, *you* will know that *she* knows. And so I switched from the symbolic language to plain English. I said to her, "Your mommy will never again eat dinner with you at the kitchen table and will never again walk with you in the park. To me that means that your mommy is not going to get well. To me that means that she's going to die." And she looked at me and said, "Yes!" implying, "What took you so long?" *(amusement in audience)*

And it is in that language... and that is how I mean it when I say, "You do not tell *them*. They always, and I mean always, tell *you* — if you understand their language."

I asked her what it meant to her that her mommy was going to die, and she said very quickly, "My mommy is going to Heaven." Then I said, "What does *that* mean to you?" And she closed her mouth very tight, took a step back and curtly said, "I don't know."

How many of you in this audience — if you try to behave like Americans for two minutes, and that means not to be shy *(amusement in audience)* — how many of you would say to two children like these with a dying mother something to the effect, "Your mommy is going to Heaven"? *(silence in audience)*

Be a bit honest and put your hands up! *(coughing and uneasiness in audience)*

I see two hands. Would you believe that only two of you would do that? *(laughs and coughing)* Do you believe that?

If two kids with a mother who will die within two days asked you, "What is going to happen to my mommy when she dies?" How many of you in some way or other would say, "Your mommy will go to Heaven."? *(stirs in audience)*

Now we got about thirty hands! And if I kept on asking you another ten times I would slowly be coming close to the right answer *(laughs)*. I am trying to show this to you. And this is true everywhere in the world.

How many would never, ever, ever say, "Your mommy goes to Heaven"? *(A short silence. No hands. Amusement.)* That is the accurate number. Usually.

The reason why I am trying to show that to you is that most people, if they are honest and not afraid to say the wrong thing in public, would admit that. That is the most frequent statement that grown ups make to children. And that answer implies that your mommy is going to a good place where there is no more pain, no more suffering. That is really why you say it. But it *also* means, "Would you please shut up now! Don't ask any more questions and go out and play!" We don't admit that, but that is true.

What we grownups imply to those children is, "Your mommy goes to a good place where there is no more pain, no more suffering." And we hope that we convey that to those children. And the next day when mommy dies, the same grown ups cry and carry on like the greatest tragedy had happened. Do you understand why your children do not believe you?

This has been the biggest problem.

I told Lorrie, "I'm not going to talk about Heaven. I think that it's terribly

important that you know what happens
to your mommy right now. Your mommy
is in a coma. A coma means that your
mommy is like a cocoon. The cocoon
looks like it's dead. Your mother cannot
hug you any more. She cannot talk to you
any more. She cannot respond to you any
more. But she *hears* every single word you
say. And very soon, in a day or two, what
is going to happen to your mommy is
what happens to a butterfly. When the
time is right the cocoon opens up and the
butterfly comes out." (That is the symbolic, verbal language.)

And we talked about butterflies and
cocoons. She asked a lot of questions
about mommy, and I asked the physician
to break a rule — in American hospitals,
children are not allowed to make visits.
We called up and received permission
from a very loving physician; he would
smuggle those children into the hospital.

And I asked them if they wanted to see
mommy once more to say all the things
that they needed to say before mommy
would die. The children very angrily said,

"They won't let us," and I said, "Would you bet?" (That's how I win all my bets nowadays.)

We believe very strongly that it is better to bring flowers to people during their lifetime than to pile them up on their casket. We believe very strongly that if people love music they should have music at a time like this. I asked the children for their mommy's favorite music. Their mommy loved John Denver. So we gave the children tapes with John Denver.

＊＊＊

My consultation was over in about forty-five minutes. It was a lovely time spent, and it had incredible consequences. The teacher called up the next day and cried over the telephone and said that it was the most moving visit she had ever made to a hospital.

She had opened the door to the hospital room, and there was this mother in a coma. Her husband was sitting *this* far away from the bed (*Elisabeth spreads her arms very wide*), a picture of total loneliness. Nobody touching.

The two little girls dashed into the room, jumped up on mommy's bed and with great joy and delight — they were not morbid and depressed and unhappy — they shared with mommy that they knew that she could not hug them any more, but that she could hear every word they said and that very soon, like in a day or two, she would be as free as a butterfly.

The father naturally started to sob and cry and finally hugged his children and communicated with them. The teacher, very appropriately, left them alone for some private, intimate sharing.

In the United States school system we have something called 'show and tell.' Children bring something special to school and are allowed to share that with the class.

The next morning Lorrie went to 'show and tell' in school. She went up to the blackboard, drew a cocoon and a butterfly coming out of the cocoon and shared with her class of first graders her visit to her dying mommy in the hospital, and thus gave what we considered the first Death and Dying Seminar to a class of first graders by a first grader. The only one who cried through the whole session was the school teacher.

The children began to open up and to share with Lorrie experiences of deaths in their own lives, usually the death of a pet, of a beloved animal, and sometimes of a grandma or a grandpa.

Because of this one shared moment with her mother, this child was able to reach the whole class of first graders.

But that's not all there is to it. What I try to share with you is that if you spend one hour with a child and share with her the experiences of death, it has the most incredible ramifications. Because without that hour I would not be here in Stockholm tonight.

In January, when I came back from Switzerland, I looked at my enormous pile of letters which, after Christmas with the Christmas cards, grows into the thousands and thousands. When I procrastinate, I always go to the kitchen and bake Christmas cookies for another day. I do that in May and August also *(amusement in audience)*. I looked at this enormous pile of unanswered mail and decided, "No. I just can't do that again." I decided to retire. I headed toward the kitchen and then I looked back at the pile once more and saw this big, yellow Manila envelope with the kind of big printed letters that little children write. I opened it up and I baked no more Christmas cookies that year!

It was a gift from Lorrie. Her letter said, "Dear Dr. Ross, I would like to give you a consultation fee." She described how she was thinking about what she would give me, what would be meaningful, and she decided that she was going to give me the most precious gift that any child could ever, ever, ever give me. She gave me the whole collection of all the condolence letters that she had received from her classmates the next day when her mommy died. Every single letter was a drawing by a first grader with two or three lines written on it.

One letter said, "Dear Lorrie, I am very sad that your mommy died, but I guess it is only the shedding of a physical body, and maybe it was simply time to shed. Love, so and so." *(amusement in audience)*

What I am trying to convey to you is that if we grownups would be more honest, and instead of making such an incredible nightmare out of dying, we could convey to children where we are at and what we feel; if we would not be embarrassed to shed tears or to express our anger and rage (if we have any), and if we would not try to shield our children from the windstorms of life but instead share with them, then the children of the next generation will not have such a horrible problem about death and dying.

The Boy in San Diego

If you sit with a child and care for him, and if you are not afraid of his answers, then he will tell you practically everything about himself.

A few months ago I was in a bakery in San Diego to get some bread. I looked through the glass window and I saw a tiny little boy sitting on the curb. He looked *very* sad. I just had to go out and sit with him.

I sat there about half an hour without saying a word. I didn't move close to him, because I just knew that if I came on too fast too soon, he would take off.

After about half an hour I said, short and matter of factly, something like, "It's tough." He said, "Uh huh."

After another fifteen minutes I said something like, "That bad?" He said, "Yes, I'm running away from home."

After another five minutes I said again, "*That* bad?" And without saying one single word he lifted his T-shirt up, and his whole chest — I dropped my jaw — his whole chest was covered with burns from a hot iron. Front and back.

All this was symbolic, nonverbal language. I can sit for forty-five minutes you see, like a dog catcher, and I really care and sit with them and give them the space they need to share with me.

Interpretation of Children's Drawings

Older children write spontaneous poems, which is also the language of the soul, or they do collages to convey to you something that they cannot put into words. If you would be more honest — more like children — and if you don't understand what they try to convey to you, you say, "I don't understand. Explain it to me." Then they will explain it to you.

But if you just look at the collage and say, "Oh, that's nice!" and think that it is nothing, then you will miss the opportunity to understand what the child wanted to say to you. Some time ago they brought me my absolutely most incredible example of that, made by a fifteen year old girl.

It is my saddest but most practical example of symbolic, nonverbal language. I want all of you to see it. It's a collage. This fifteen year old girl asked everybody in the family to look at her collage, and she also asked the social worker. Nobody cared and took time enough to really look at it. And if any one of those people would have looked at it and understood the symbolic, nonverbal language, then this child would be alive today.

After having passed this collage around for two weeks, she committed suicide.

After she had committed suicide, the social worker sent me her collage saying, "Isn't that a wonderful example!"

Do you understand that this is very sad to me? It is so sad that this child had to die before the social worker learned to hear and listen to the girl's efforts to share her anguish and agony.

The Four Quadrants

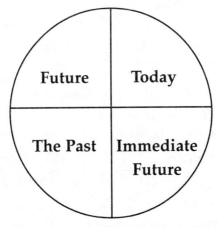

The four quadrants of a drawing according to Jung

I will point out some details in this collage for you.

It is very easy to read this collage. You don't have to be a psychiatrist, you don't have to "psychoanalyze" what you see. All you have to do is very simply to look at it, knowing a few basic things. Then you will understand how much all of us, and I mean everybody in here, how much all of us know inside. But up here *(indicating head)* you have only limited knowledge or awareness. If you want to get in touch with your inner knowledge which is far beyond anything you can put into words, try to get in touch with this and then you will also be able to hear your fellow man who really needs your help.

If you read this collage now you will understand that if somebody would have taken five or ten minutes time with this girl, she would probably still be alive.

According to Jung — I presume that all of you know who he was — you start looking at such a picture from the **left lower quadrant,** which is your past. And don't psychoanalyze it. Just read what it says. This girl made it easy for us. She made a combination of nonverbal, symbolic language and plain English. She even added words to it to be sure that somebody would be able understand it. Down below you read, "A suffering child needs your help." And you see a picture and what does the picture show? An ocean. What kind of an ocean? Is it a friendly inviting ocean? No, it's a dark scary ocean with no life boat and no lighthouse. There is nothing to hold on to. This is how she visually experienced her childhood. And that is scary and very, very lonely.

Then you go from there to the **right upper quadrant,** which is your today and which tells you how she felt at the moment she made this collage and what she is most afraid of today, the day she is making this collage. It says, "I'm crazy." She is afraid that she is going to be crazy. And the second biggest words are — you always start with the biggest pictures or the biggest writings and go to the smaller ones — the big question "Why?" And next to it, "Make friends with mommy." Which is the biggest image in the "now" quadrant? It's a mommy dog with puppy dogs. A family unit. The next picture is a baby clutching a doll to his chest. Then comes the smallest of the three pictures. It is a monkey who monkeys around. What do monkeys who monkey around stand for? It's like a clown who clowns to cover up his sadness. What does a monkey or a clown tell you about the prognosis? Anybody who can still monkey around has a chance because she still has a sense of humor. So she could still have been helped.

Now what is going to happen to her next week? The **right lower quadrant** is the immediate future. And what is going to happen in the immediate future to this fifteen year old girl? What are the words? "Fight to be free." And then, "Free again," and then, "Tough choice." And what is the image of her anticipated existence in a week from now? You see a forest where a big part of the forest has been chopped down already. In terms of prognosis: a glimpse of hope because there are new trees coming in the foreground. But what happens to the same monkey who a week earlier still monkeyed around? What is he doing now? He has stopped monkeying around. He is paralyzed. He is just sitting there numb, not playing anymore.

And then you go to the **left upper quadrant,** which is your concept of death and what you anticipate the future to hold. And that tells you how internally, from her spiritual, intuitive quadrant, she anticipates the outcome of her present situation. And what do you see? What does she know already? It is a hospital. And what happens in a hospital? A baby is born. What kind of a delivery? It's a baby that the doctor holds upside down. When do you hold babies upside down? When they don't scream, when they don't breathe. She already knew when she made this collage that she would be found not breathing and her hope was that she would get into the hands of a competent doctor who would bring her back to breathing. That is how you read those collages.

If that is not happening, what is the next biggest picture? A cat. What do cats stand for? Nine lives. If a doctor cannot bring you back to life, maybe there is something to what some people believe —that we have more lives than one. And if that is not possible, what is her last hope? I mean this collage tells you everything! What is the last picture? It's a lighthouse. You see down here in the left lower quadrant there is an ocean with no lighthouse. Up here it's a lighthouse of what some people experience: the light at the end of the tunnel. That is how you read those pictures.

⚜

You cannot get a more classical cry for help than this one, and it is even easy to see where the problem lies. But nobody saw it and that is the tragedy. When she was found, she had the collage with her, and, needless to say, the social worker felt very guilty for not having taken time out to look at it and to help her. And they sent it to me and asked me to promise that I would show it to all the grownups wherever they were listening to me. And if you forget the whole collage that's very OK, but do look at it and if another teenager who is suicidal or desperate gives you a collage, sit down and ask and he or she will be very glad that you cared enough to at least ask.

And that is essentially what we need to learn. To take time out for things that are essential. For being able to listen to our fellow man and for being able to hear what he has to say are essential. And also to learn the humility that if you don't understand what they are trying to tell us, then it is OK to say, "I don't know what you are saying. Can you rephrase it?" And once you open up the communication, you will find that it is not half as difficult as you thought that it would be.

Liz

Some time ago I was called to a twelve-year-old who was dying. We were able to take her home to die. I take all my children home to die if humanly possible. But we never put them in the bedroom because bedrooms are often used to punish children. I presume that it is not different here in Sweden. I think that you all remember that when you were naughty as a child you were sent to your bedroom and when you shaped up you were allowed to come out again. So many children associate the bedrooms with no-nos, taboos, punishment, and isolation.

Therefore, we take them into the living room in a big bed where they can see the forest, the garden, the clouds or the flowers, the birds, or the snow.

Liz was in a bed in the living room; very, very slowly dying of cancer. The mother was able to reach the girl in a very nice way. But the father was unable to say anything — he was an introvert and was incapable of talking about anything at all. But he was able to *show* her his love. He used to buy and bring home red roses, which he put on her table without a word. The whole family were very orthodox Catholics.

The father insisted that the other children (six, ten and eleven years old) did not know that their sister was dying. I did not believe that. I finally received permission from the father to see those children alone after school and have them draw a picture.

They drew pictures and it was very clear that they knew. Again, it was the six-year-old who started to switch from symbolic language to plain English. He said, "Yeah, she is going to die very soon." I said, "You know Peter, Liz is going to die in a day or two probably. If you have any unfinished business with her, do it now. Because you will feel much, much better if you don't postpone it until it is too late." Then he said, "Well, I am supposed to tell her I love her." I said, "No! You are not supposed to tell her 'I love you'. That is phony. You obviously have a lot of negative feelings inside, the way you sound."

And he finally blurted out, "Yeah. Sometimes I am terribly tired of her. I wish that she had dropped dead already." I said, "Yes, it has taken a long time. How come you're so impatient?" He said, "Well, I can't watch television, I can't slam the door, I can't bring friends home." Very natural things for a six year old. I was standing there helping him to say those things.

I told them that all children have the same feelings that he had, but only a few of them are brave enough to admit it. And now we were sitting here together and had the courage to say whatever we wanted to say. And you can be sure that they talked to their heart's content. It was fantastic.

I finally said to him, "I wonder if you're the only really honest person who can share that with your sister?" But he was already contaminated by the grown-ups so he said, "One ought not to say those things." I said, "You truly believe that if you feel and think those things, that your sister does not know it? How much more beautiful would it be if you could lovingly share that with her! And what a relief for her that somebody would really be open and loving with her."

I challenged him to it and he finally said that he would try.

We walk into this room. There is the bed. The six-year-old is next to his dying sister. I am behind him, ready to give him a little push if necessary. Behind me is the ten-year-old, then the eleven-year-old. From the door the mother appears, and behind the mother, the father. In chronological order of comfort! (*giggles from audience*)

The boy finally, after a little procrastination, blurted out: "Sometimes I wished I could pray to get it over with." And the moment he said that the most beautiful consultation experience I had had in a long time happened. His twelve year old dying sister started to sob and sob and sob and cry. Not tears of pain, but of the greatest relief.

And she said, "Thank God, thank God, thank God, thank God, thank God!"

And then, when she recuperated from her tears, she finally explained why she felt this great relief. She said, "You know Peter, for the last three days and three nights already I have prayed to God to take me away. And every time I finish my prayer Mom comes in, stands at the door and tells me that she has been sitting up all night praying to God to keep me alive. But if you help me, Peter, we can outdo Mom." *(laughter from audience)*

Liz was so happy that they finally had stopped pretending, and they all hugged each other. And you understand that the six year old was the proudest young man in town, with the biggest, proudest grin on his face. And the beauty was that the mother heard her daughter saying that.

With this, the greatest problem was solved: both the parents and the children were prepared.

But Liz cold not die. For some reason she hung on to life. Three days later I went back. Medically speaking, it was incomprehensible that she was still hanging in there. I said to the mother, "She should have died at least a week ago. She is ready for it, she wants it, but she can't let go. I have tried everything. There is something that holds her back from letting go. I think that there is something that scares her. If it is OK with you, I am just going to ask her a straightforward question. But I want you to come with me, so you won't be worried over what I might have said to her. I want you to hear it yourself."

I said, "Liz, you can't die, can you?" And she said, "No."

I said, "How come?" She said, "Because I can't get to Heaven." Very surprised, I said, "Who told you that?"

The biggest problem with this kind of consultation is that, in trying to help one human being, you discover that you have to attack another one. It is very difficult to stop doing that, because you come across so much quackery, so much rubbish, so much scary nonsense that dying patients are told — in short, so much negativity, that it is very difficult not to become negative yourself.

Therefore I restrained myself when I asked her, "Who told you that?"

She told me that the priests and the nuns and the sisters who used to come to

see her had told her many, many times
that no one gets to Heaven unless she has
loved God more than anybody else in the
whole wide world. And then she leaned
up again and with her skinny fingers that
were . . . her arms were like sticks of chalk
and her belly looked like it was nine
months pregnant. She tried to lean up at
me and literally hang on to me and she
whispered in my ear to prevent God from
hearing her. She whispered in my ear,
"You understand Dr. Ross, I love my
mommy and daddy more than anybody
else in the whole wide world." I was on
the point of crying.

I find this incredibly sad. And the question is: how do you help a child like this?
You *could* say nice words — and it would
not help. You *could* say, "By loving
mommy and daddy you also love God,"
or things to that effect — and it would
not help. How do you help her to get rid
of her feelings of guilt?

The only thing that works is for you to
acknowledge *your own* negativity. We call
it "the Hitler within us": when we get

nasty, when we get critical, when we get judgmental, when we label people, when we don't like other people's methods.

And I was very angry at that priest who did that to Liz and at those nuns and sisters who use fear and guilt with little children.

But you understand, this is *my* problem, not Liz's problem.

So I told her, "I am not getting into an argument who is right and who is wrong. I'm only going to talk to you the way I always have."

That means I will now — for my own sake — go home and look at why I'm so critical, and put it temporarily into a drawer. But sooner or later I will have to deal with it so it does not interfere with my work. *Because you cannot do one positive thing to somebody in this world if you do it by knocking somebody else.*

I then used the symbolic verbal language. (It is the biggest gift to be able to use that language.) I said to her, "You and I have always talked about school. You were a very great honor student. The biggest dream in your life has always been to become a teacher. And the only time since I learned to know you that I ever saw you devastated was in September when the school year started and the school bus came and you looked through the window and you saw your friends and your brothers and sisters getting up on the school bus."

One month earlier she had been told that she was cured, but just before school started they had discovered the first metastases. I went on, "And I think for the first time in your life, it hit you that you would never, ever again be on that school bus, that you would never again be able to go to your beloved school, that you would never become a teacher."

And she said, "Yes."

I said, "I want you to answer me one single question. Sometimes it happens that your teacher gives *very* tough assignments. Does she give these super tough assignments to her worst students? What I would like to know is if she gives these assignments to the worst pupils in the class, or if she gives them to just anybody in the class. Or does she give them only to very few of her best, chosen students?"

Then her face lit up — I have never seen anything like it — and she said, "Oh, she gives them to *very* few of us." She was one of the best pupils in her class and was very proud of it. And I said: "Since God is also a teacher, what do you think: did He give you a tough assignment, or did He give you one that He could have given to just any child in the class?"

Then again, in the symbolic, nonverbal language, she looked down at her poor, devastated body — her *very* huge belly and her very skinny arms and legs. She looked down at her body like she was evaluating the tests of her life. Then she smiled a happy smile and dead seriously she said, "I don't think God could give a tougher assignment to any child."

And I didn't have to add, "What do you *now* think that He thinks of you?"

The last nonverbal communication I had with Liz was a few days later when I went back, more to see how the other children were doing.

She was slipping into a semiconscious state. I stood under the doorway, taking a last look at her, really to say good-bye to her in a silent way. She suddenly opened her eyes, obviously recognized me, and again with this big, almost smirk, almost happy grin on her face, she looked down at her belly like, "I got your message."

This is how we try to help children to finish their unfinished business. It is very easy to work with dying patients. It is even more easy to work with dying children because they are less complicated. They are very straightforward. And the beauty, the incredible beauty about children is that when you make a boo-boo they give you instant feedback. If you make a mistake you know it immediately.

We will try to teach the symbolic language not only to medical students, but to seminary students, to teachers and to nurses, so that they can better learn to understand the language of the ones who are in most need of their help.

Those of you who have children: listen, really listen to your children and you will learn a language that is more important than Esperanto or English or Spanish or any world language because it is the language of the needy people. And the exchange that you get for learning it are gifts to help you to live fully.

When you listen to dying patients who have been able to finish their unfinished business, you will find that for the first time in their life they learn what it means to live fully.

Dougy

A few years ago I was giving a lecture in Virginia. You may not know this, but I hate lecturing. It is terrible to stand on the stage, you know, day after day, basically saying the same things. And in those days I used to lecture from nine A.M. to five P.M. So I needed some fuel. My fuel was to read the audience to see if there was somebody interesting there; you know, I guess who they are and what they are doing. It's . . . it's a game that I play.

That particular day I was looking around the audience saying to myself, "You will have to talk to this group all day." In the front row sat a couple. The moment I looked at them I had this incredible urge — which you understand does not come from the intellectual part of one's self but from the intuitive, spiritual part — to ask them why in the world they hadn't brought their child to my lecture.

Well *(she laughs a little),* I would say that a normal psychiatrist doesn't do that. I don't think that exists *(laughter from audience).* I mean, you don't say a thing like that from the stage while you are giving a lecture. I really had to control myself not to ask them. If I had, people naturally would have said that I was crazy. But on the other hand, other people's opinion of me is their problem, not mine. Right?

But I made a physiologic break very early — much too early — and I went to this couple. They were very down-to-earth, regular people. I phrased my question in a socially acceptable way, saying, "I don't know why I need to say this, but I have this urge to ask you: why didn't you bring your child here?"

And they didn't laugh at me. They just looked at me and said, "It's interesting that you should say that, because we debated early this morning if we should bring him, but the problem is that today is the day of his chemotherapy."

As you can see, their answer already confirmed to me: yes they have a child, it is a boy, he has cancer and he is on chemotherapy. I said, "I don't know why I am saying this, but it is very urgent that he be here."

They knew unconditional love, and the father left during the break. About eleven o'clock he came back with his adorable nine-year-old boy who was wide-eyed, very pale, and totally bald from the treatment. They all sat in the front row. The boy took in every word I said.

And the father gave him a box of Crayola and a piece of paper. To keep him quiet, *he* thought. To *me,* it was divine manipulation, not chance.

At the twelve o'clock lunch break — it was the usual chicken lunch, which I have five times a week so I skip it *(laughter from audience)* — he came up with his Crayola picture and said, "Dr. Ross, this is a present for you." I thanked him and looked at it and... I am a translator, to translate is my main job, so I looked at his picture and I said to him without thinking (this little guy wasn't there when I was talking about the drawings) I said to him, "Shall we tell 'em?"

He immediately knew what I was talking about. He looked at his parents and said, "Yes, I think so." I said, "Everything?" He looked at them again and said, "Yes, I think that they can take it."

Nine-year-old children who have a terminal illness are wise, old souls. All children are very old, wise souls if they have suffered, if their physical body has deteriorated before adolescence. God created man in such a miraculous way that the spiritual aspect, which usually does not emerge until adolescence, begins to emerge prematurely to compensate for the loss of the physical abilities. This is why young dying children are very old, wise souls if you understand that symbolically speaking. They are much wiser than children who are healthy and have been raised in a greenhouse. That is why we always tell parents, "Do not protect your children! Share your anguish and your pain with them. Otherwise they will develop into cripples. Because sooner or later the plants have to come out of the greenhouse anyway and then they cannot withstand the cold and the winds."

So I looked at his picture, and because I am in town only one night, usually I don't want to open up something or hurt somebody and then not be available the next day. So I always double-check. And I didn't trust the mother. She looked very vulnerable. So that is why I asked the boy, "Shall we tell them all of it?" Do you understand what we were talking about?

"Shall I read your picture to your parents?"

He looked at them again and said, "Yeah, I think that they can take it." I still didn't trust the mother so I asked her, "What is your biggest, biggest fear?" She started to cry and said, "We were just told that he has three months to live."

I looked at Dougy's picture and said, "Three months? No. Impossible. Out of the question. Three years maybe. But three months is totally out of the question."

She hugged me and kissed me and thanked me. I said, "Don't do that. I am a translator and a catalyst. It is your son who knows those things. I am only translating his inner knowledge. I am not responsible for giving you three years of your child's life."

We became very fast friends. During the afternoon lecturing I watched him like a hawk. About a quarter to five he started to get sleepy. I stopped my lecture because *I* wanted to say good-bye to him. The last thing I said to him was, "Dougy,

I cannot make house calls in Virginia very often. But if you ever need me, the only thing you have to do is to write. And because I'm always a thousand letters behind, write the envelope yourself. You see, children's letters are always priority number one. And to be on the safe side write 'personal' on it." And I spelled it out to him.

I am at home only one day a week and most of the time I only have time to go through the children's letters. Grown-ups have misused that fact since. They have imitated children's writing by printing on the envelopes. If any grownups do that I refuse to answer because that is misusing my trust and that would in the end only feed into negativity.

Anyway, I waited and waited and no letter came, and you know how your head begins to interfere. I said, "Oh my God suppose he has died, I gave the parents false hope, and I . . ." I mean the whole head trip. And the longer your head trips are the more you become worried and negative. But one day I decided,

"That's ridiculous. My intuition is *very* accurate and my head is very *not* accurate many times. So forget your worries!"

And the day after I let go of my worries I had a letter from him. It was the most beautiful letter I have ever received during my twenty years of working with dying patients. It was a two liner, "Dear Dr. Ross, I have only one more question left. What is life and what is death and why do little children have to die? Love, Dougy."

Do you understand why I am prejudiced for children? They cut through all the baloney *(laughter)*. So I wrote him a letter and I couldn't write him, you know, big stuff. I had to write to him the way he wrote to me.

So I borrowed my daughter's gorgeous felt tip pens in twenty-eight colors, marvelous colors, and folded a paper up and then I folded another paper and it finally ended up in a little booklet all printed in rainbow colors, every letter a different color. It looked very pretty, but it still didn't look finished so I started to illustrate it. And then it was ready to be mailed off.

Then I had a problem. I liked it *(laughter from audience)*. And I really liked it so much that I wanted to keep it and my head immediately came to my rescue. You see, after death you know that the highest goal in life is to always take your highest choice. To keep the letter for myself wouldn't have been my highest choice but my head came to my rescue and said, "You are entitled to keep it. You can use it for your house calls with dying children. It will help the brothers and sisters of the dying child." And the longer the excuses became, the more I knew that I'd better go to the post office fast.

So I finally said to myself, "No. I'm not going to wait twenty-four hours in order to copy it. I'm gonna send it off right now, because if he dies now and the letter arrives too late, I will feel very bad. And I really made it for him, not for me."

I let go of it and mailed it.

The rewards always come back a thousand times if you take the highest choice.

Because a few months later — it was last March — he called up long distance from Virginia to California and said, "I wanted to give you a birthday gift for my birthday." And he told me that he had showed it to so many parents of dying children, and all of them wanted a copy, and therefore he decided that he would give me permission to print it, so that I could make it available to other children.

We have printed it and we call it *The Dougy Letter*.

Now I'll show you how horrible it is when you are not honest. Even with good motivations you will always get into trouble sooner or later. Some months ago I was called to a very, very famous talk show in New York City, where you talk for three minutes to ten million people and can't even say one important thing, because you have such a short time. They ask you one question and you answer it and then you are off the air. I have always wondered why people do that. But I did it too.

And instead of asking me what I wanted to say in three minutes that would be meaningful, they asked me about the five year old Jamie, who is in my book *To Live Until We Say Good-Bye*. The next day I got a very angry letter from Dougy. He wrote, "I don't understand you. Why did you have to talk about Jamie? Why couldn't you talk about me? Because if all those people had bought one *Dougy Letter* I would have been able to see my daddy again."

His daddy has, like most Americans, $200,000 debts for doctor and hospital bills. And in order to pay those bills he moonlights and has double jobs and has a weekend job as well. He very seldom has time to see his boy.

I don't think that here in Sweden you are aware of the kind of problems associated with terminal illnesses. You see, the big mistake I made was that when the family didn't have enough money to eat, I sent them a check. And in order not to make it look like a welfare check I made the mistake to write on the check, "For royalties." I made them believe that this was from the sales of *Dougy Letters*. And now this poor child expects to get such a check every six months. And I am in real trouble *(laughter from audience)*.

So every patient you work with is teaching you something, and it is not always that it has to do with death and dying, but with life and living.

The Meaning of Suffering

Dying patients, when you take your time and sit with them, teach you about the stages of dying. When you know that you are going to die soon, you go through the denial and the anger, and the "Why me?" and you question God and reject Him for a while. You bargain with Him, and you go through horrible depressions.

What does hope mean for you when you are dying? When you are told that you have a terminal illness, first you always think, "Oh, it is not true, it must be a mistake." Then you hope that it's operable or curable. If that's not true, you then hope that chemotherapy or visualization or whatever at least will take care of your symptoms and that you will be functioning and relatively healthy. Then you acknowledge that no matter how much you take in an experimental drug, you just get worse, and then you get well again and worse again. It goes up and down. Is there a point when you give up? No! There isn't a point where you give up. Whatever happens to you in terms of ups and downs, every experience that every human being in the world has is for a purpose. It will teach you one specific thing that you would otherwise not learn. And God doesn't give you any more tests than you need.

When you have passed a test you may do quite well for a while, and then something new will happen. You become blind, or your diarrhea starts again, or this or that starts again. All of us find out, you know, what is behind all this. And you fight again if you are a fighter, and if you are somebody who resigns very quickly, then you resign very quickly, but the trouble is not going to go away. So if you can find behind the trouble what you can learn...

And if you have another human being who cares, you may be able to reach a stage of acceptance.

But that is not just typical of dying; really it has nothing to do with dying. We only call it the "stages of dying" for lack of a better word. If you lose a boyfriend or a girlfriend or if you lose your job, or if you are moved from your home where you have lived for fifty years and you have to go to a nursing home, and even if you only lose a parakeet or your contact lenses, you may go through the same stages of dying.

This is, I think, the meaning of suffering: all the hardships that you face in life, all the tests and tribulations, all the nightmares and all the losses, are still viewed as curses by most people, as punishments by God, as something negative. If you would only know that nothing that comes to you is negative! I mean nothing. All the trials and tribulations and the biggest losses that you ever experience, things that make you say, "If I had known about this, I would never have been able to make it through," are gifts to you. It is like somebody who has to...*(turns to audience)* What do you call it when you make the hot iron into a tool? You have to temper the iron.

Every hardship is an opportunity that you are given, an opportunity to grow. To grow is the sole purpose of existence on this planet Earth. You will not grow if you sit in a beautiful flower garden and somebody brings you gorgeous food on a silver platter. But you will grow if you are sick, if you are in pain, if you experience losses and still don't put your head in the sand, but take the pain and learn to accept it, not as a curse or a punishment, but as a gift to you with a very, very specific purpose.

I will now give you a clinical example of that. In one of my one-week workshops — they are one-week live-in retreats — there was a young woman. She did not have to face the death of a child, but she faced several what we call "little deaths," although not very little in her own eyes. When she gave birth to a second baby girl, which she was very much looking forward to, she was told in a not very humane way that the child was severely retarded. In fact the child would never even be able to recognize her as a mother. When she became aware of this, her husband walked out on her. Suddenly she was faced with a very difficult situation. She had two young, very needy, very dependent children, and she had no money, no income and no help.

She went through a terrible denial. She couldn't even use the word "retardation."

After that she went through a fantastic anger at God and cursed him out. First He didn't exist at all. Then He was a mean old... you know what. After that she went through a tremendous bargaining — if the child at least would be educable, or at least could recognize her as a mother. Then she found some genuine meaning in having this child, and I will simply share with you how she finally resolved her problem. It began to dawn on her that nothing in life is a coincidence. She tried to look at this child and tried to figure out what purpose a little vegetable-like human being could have on this Earth. Finally she found the solution, and I am sharing this with you in the form of a poem that she wrote. She is not a poet, but still it is very moving. In the poem she identifies with her child who talks to her godmother. She calls the poem "To My Godmother."

To My Godmother

What is a godmother?
I know you're very special.
You waited many months for my arrival.
You were there and saw me when only
                    minutes old,
and changed my diapers when I had
            been there just a few days.
You had dreams of your first godchild.
She would be precocious like your sister,
You'd see her off to school, college, and
                    marriage.

*How would I turn out? A credit to those
who have me?*

God had other plans for me. I'm just me.

*No one ever used the word precocious
about me.*

*Something hasn't hooked up right in my
mind.*

I'll be a child of God for all time.

*I'm happy. I love everyone, and they love
me.*

There aren't many words I can say,

*But I can communicate and understand
affection, warmth, softness and love.*

There are special people in my life.

*Sometimes I sit and smile and some
times cry.*

I wonder why?

I am happy and loved by special friends.

What more could I ask for?

*Oh sure, I'll never go to college, or
marry.*

*But don't be sad. God made me very
special.*

I cannot hurt. Only love.

And maybe God needs some children
*   who simply love.*
Do you remember when I was baptized,
You held me, hoping I wouldn't cry and
*   you wouldn't drop me?*
Neither happened and it was a very
*   happy day.*
Is that why you are my godmother?
I know you are soft and warm, give me
*   love,*
but there is something very special in
*   your eyes.*
I see that look and feel that love from
*   others.*
I must be special to have so many
*   mothers.*
No, I will never be a success in the eyes
*   of the world,*
But I promise you something very few
*   people can.*
Since all I know is love, goodness and
*   innocence,*
Eternity will be ours to share, my
*   godmother.*

This is the same mother who, a few months before, was willing to let her toddler crawl out near the swimming pool while pretending to go to the kitchen so the child would fall into the swimming pool and drown. A tremendous change has taken place in this mother.

This is what takes place in all of you if you are willing always to look at what happens in your life from both sides. There is never just one side to it. You may be terminally ill, you may have a lot of pain, you may not find somebody to talk to about it. You may feel that it is unfair to take you away in the middle of your life, that you have not really started to live yet. Then look at the other side of the coin and you are suddenly one of the few fortunate people who are able to throw overboard all the baloney that you have carried with you in your life.

When you have done that, you will be able to go to somebody and say, "I love you" when he can still hear it, and after that you can skip the schmaltzy eulogies. And as you know that you are here for a very short time, you can finally do the things that you really want to do. How many of you in this room do exactly what you love to do? I mean *totally* live? *(a very few hands)* How many do not? *(more hands)* Would you change your work on Monday? *(laughter)*

It is very important that you only do what you love to do. You may be poor, you may go hungry, you may lose your car, you may have to move into a shabby place to live, but you will *totally* live. And at the end of your days you will bless your life because you have done what you came here to do. Otherwise, you will live as a prostitute, you will do things only for a reason, to please other people, and you will never have lived. And you will not have a pleasant death.

If on the other hand you listen to your own inner voice, to your own inner wisdom, which is far greater than anybody else's as far as you are concerned, you will not go wrong and you will know what to do with your life. Then time is no longer relevant.

The hardest lesson that people have to learn is to learn unconditional love. And that is very hard to learn. Virginia Satir, whom some of you may know, described very beautifully what unconditional love is all about. She says:

I want to love you without clutching,
appreciate you without judging,
join you without invading,
invite you without demanding,
leave you without guilt,
evaluate you without blaming
and help you without insulting.
If I can have the same from you,
then we can truly meet and enrich each
                                    other.